Psychiatry - Theory, Applications and Treatments

DATE DUE

Co   IN

C   D

PSYCHIATRY - THEORY, APPLICATIONS AND TREATMENTS

Attention Deficit Hyperactivity Disorder (ADHD)
Stuart M. Gordon and Aileen E. Mitchell (Editors)
Book Description:
2009. 978-1-60741-581-7

War and Suicide
Leo Sher and Alexander Vilens (Editors)
2009. 978-1-60741-978-5

**Stress of Family Members in Caring
for a Relative with Schizophrenia**
Wai-Tong Chien (Author)
2009. 978-1-60876-145-6

Attention Deficit Hyperactivity Disorder (ADHD)
Stuart M. Gordon and Aileen E. Mitchell (Editors)
2009. 978-1-60876-699-4

War and Suicide
Leo Sher and Alexander Vilens (Editors)
2009. 978-1-61668-274-3

Victimhood, Vengefulness, and the Culture of Forgiveness
Ivan Urlić, Miriam Berger and Avi Berman (Authors)
2010. 978-1-60876-191-3

**Psychiatric Research Trends:
Dreams and Geriatric Psychiatry**
Daniella M. Montez (Editor)
2010. 978-1-60741-760-6

Cognitive Impairment in Children with ADHD
Alasdair Vance, Catherine Mollica
and Paul Maruff (Authors)
2010. 978-1-61668-476-1

Post-Traumatic Stress Disorder (PTSD):
Causes, Symptoms and Treatment
Sylvia J. Egan (Editor)
2010. 978-1-61668-716-8

Psychiatric Research Trends:
Dreams and Geriatric Psychiatry
Daniella M. Montez (Editor)
2010. 978-1-61668-719-9

Neurobiology of Post-Traumatic Stress Disorder
Leo Sher and Alexander Vilens (Editors)
2010.

Dyslexia and Depression: The Hidden Sorrow
Neil Alexander-Passe (Author)
2010. 978-1-61668-933-9

Psychiatry - Theory, Applications and Treatments

Cognitive Impairment in Children with ADHD

Alasdair Vance, Catherine Mollica and Paul Maruff

Nova Science Publishers, Inc.

New York

For permission to use material from this book please contact us:
Telephone 631-231-7269; Fax 631-231-8175
Web Site: http://www.novapublishers.com

NOTICE TO THE READER

LIBRARY OF CONGRESS CATALOGING-IN-PUBLICATION DATA

Vance, Alasdair.
  Cognitive impairment in children with ADHD / Alasdair Vance, Catherine Mollica, and Paul Maruff.
      p. ; cm.
  Includes bibliographical references and index.
  ISBN 978-1-61668-197-5 (softcover)
  1. Attention-deficit hyperactivity disorder--Chemotherapy--Complications.
  2. Cognitive disorders in children--Treatment. 3. Cognition in children--Testing. I. Mollica, Catherine. II. Maruff, Paul. III. Title.
  [DNLM: 1. Attention Deficit Disorder with Hyperactivity--drug therapy. 2. Central Nervous System Stimulants. 3. Child. 4. Cognition--drug effects.
  5. Dose-Response Relationship, Drug. 6. Psychological Tests. WS 350.8.A8 V222c 2010]
  RJ506.H9V35 2010
  618.92'8589--dc22
                                        2010012177

Published by Nova Science Publishers, Inc. † New York

CONTENTS

PREFACE

There is limited understanding of the problems associated with repeated neuropsychological assessment in children, including the statistics used to guide decisions about cognitive change. Further, clinicians rarely consider change in cognitive function when evaluating treatment response in individual children with ADHD. This is most likely due to a lack of suitable assessment tasks as well as clinicians' limited awareness of the appropriate statistical techniques for measuring cognitive change in individuals. This book outlines a study investigating the application of a statistically principled decision rule to the cognitive and behavioural measures of individual children with ADHD in order to classify a significant, positive response to medication.

Chapter 1

INTRODUCTION

There is limited understanding of the problems associated with repeated neuropsychological assessment in children, including the statistics used to guide decisions about cognitive change. Further, clinicians rarely consider change in cognitive function when evaluating treatment response in individual children with ADHD. This is most likely due to a lack of suitable assessment tasks as well as clinicians' limited awareness of the appropriate statistical techniques for measuring cognitive change in individuals. This chapter outlines a study investigating the application of a statistically principled decision rule to the cognitive and behavioural measures of individual children with ADHD in order to classify a significant, positive response to medication. The data demonstrate an evidence-based approach to clinical decision-making that can be used to evaluate cognitive and behavioural improvement in individual children with ADHD following treatment with stimulant medication. Then, a study investigating a novel "intensive design" method for assessing stimulant medication-related improvement in cognitive function in children with ADHD is presented. The results demonstrate the effectiveness of the medication in improving behavioural symptoms of ADHD, as well as certain features of cognitive function (psychomotor, visual attention and learning). Overall, these findings support the use of a novel "intensive" within-subjects design to examine the short-term effects of stimulant medication on cognitive and behavioural functions in children with ADHD. Further, this design is readily utilised in routine clinical practice.

Chapter 1

STUDY 1

Attention-deficit/Hyperactivity disorder (ADHD) is characterised by developmentally inappropriate levels of inattention, and/or impulsiveness/overactivity (American Psychiatric Association, 1994). Stimulant medication is currently the most common and effective treatment for this disorder (Conners et al., 2001; Hoagwood et al., 2000). Successful response to treatment with stimulant medication is typically inferred from a reduction in behavioural symptoms, as determined by clinical judgment and/or parent and teacher behavioural ratings (Aman & Turbott, 1991). Although medication-responsiveness can vary according to many factors such as the severity of ADHD symptoms, medication dose, or the presence of comorbid disorders (Buitelaar et al., 1995; Denney & Rapport, 1999; DuPaul et al., 1994), the incidence of actual non-response is reported to be rare when thorough medication trials are conducted (Elia et al., 1991). In addition to improving behavioural symptoms, there is strong evidence to suggest that performance on tests of psychomotor, attention and memory also improves following treatment with stimulant medication (e.g., Bedard et al., 2003; de Sonneville et al., 1994; Douglas et al., 1995; Douglas et al., 1986; Mollica et al., submitted; for a review, see Rapport & Kelly, 1993). These findings suggest that improvement in cognitive function may be another useful marker of treatment response in individual children with ADHD (Rapport & Denney, 2000); therefore, it is important to improve current methods of assessing and analysing cognitive change in individuals with ADHD in order to accurately measure treatment outcomes.

There are at least three reasons for the limited application of cognitive tests to assist clinical decisions about treatment response in ADHD. First, tests of cognitive function that are used by clinicians must support reliable inferences about the presence or absence of change in cognitive function in individual patients. This is in contrast to the use of neuropsychological tests in research studies, where inferences about change are based on the performance of *groups* of children, and are aimed primarily at developing brain-behaviour models of the disorder. In fact, it has been argued that the optimal characteristics of tests designed to detect cognitive change differ substantially from those of most conventional neuropsychological tests (see Collie et al., 2003; Collie et al., 2003; Silbert et al., 2004). Collie and colleagues suggest that tests that are administered repeatedly should contain equivalent alternate forms, incorporate simple response requirements, and include a brief administration time to minimise the effects of practice. In addition, it is necessary that the performance metrics of such tests incorporate features that facilitate the detection of subtle cognitive change. These include a large range of scores to allow for performance variation, and scores that yield a normal data distribution. Because decisions about individuals are generally made without reference to a matched control group, it is necessary that the effects of repeated administration on a cognitive test be minimal, or if present be understood thoroughly.

A second reason for the limited application of cognitive tests to assist clinical decisions about treatment response in ADHD concerns the analysis of data from individuals. The statistical methods required to guide decisions about cognitive improvement in individuals are not as well developed as the methods used to define cognitive impairment (typically a comparison to some normative range) or those used to compare the cognitive performance of groups of children before and after medication. However, an increasing specialisation in the identification of cognitive change, such as that which can result from concussion, has led to improved methods for guiding decisions about cognitive change in individuals (for a review, see Collie et al., 2002). These methods include Reliable Change Indices (RCIs) and related techniques (the Modified Reliable Change Indices (MRCIs) and Reliability-Stability Index), as well as simple and multiple regression techniques. However, most of these methods cannot be applied within clinical settings because they require data from some healthy comparison group tested over equivalent intervals to the patient of interest, and such data are rarely available for conventional neuropsychological tests (McCaffrey & Westervelt, 1995).

The third issue for the limited application of cognitive tests to determining treatment response relates to the aspects of cognitive function assessed. At present, simple stimulus-response tests are often used to measure change in the cognitive function of individual patients after medication (e.g., the Test of Variables of Attention (TOVA); Greenberg & Waldman, 1993; the VIGIL; Rodgers et al., 2003). Simple tests are attractive because they are generally brief (i.e., they require less than 30 minutes), deliver data that have good metric properties, and are not associated with substantial practice effects. However, as children with ADHD show impairment across a range of cognitive functions (e.g., attention, executive function, and memory; Barnett et al., 2001; Barnett et al., submitted), the measurement of single aspects of cognition may cause true medication-related improvement to be overlooked. Importantly, assessing medication effects with many different cognitive tests increases the time required for testing.

Even if the time required to assess multiple cognitive functions can be minimised there remains an important statistical issue. When the criterion for classifying change is constant (e.g., improvement >1 standard deviation), the probability of detecting improvement or decline by chance increases with the number of tests given. For example, the probability of detecting change of one standard deviation unit in cognitive function using 10 tests is much greater than the probability of detecting change using a single test. To reduce the probability of Type I error as the number of tests in a battery increases, the criterion used to define change should be made more conservative. Ingraham and Aitken (1996) have shown that the experiment-wise error rate can be controlled as the number of cognitive tests increase by increasing both the cut-off score required for a classification of change and the number of tests for which performance must exceed the cut-off score. According to their simulations, with 10 performance measures, a change rule requiring improvement greater than 1.65 SDs ($p < .05$ one-tailed) on two or more tests retains Type I error at less than.05. Another approach to controlling the experiment-wise error rate in multi-test cognitive batteries is to compute a composite score from all performance measures. The justification for this approach is that a criterion for change, such as improvement greater than 1.65 SD on at least two tests, will classify individuals as responders only if they show marked improvement in specific aspects of cognition, but not if they demonstrate subtle improvement across all or most domains. Small but positive changes across all tests will sum and increase the value of the composite score so that it can be differentiated reliably from zero (Rasmussen et al., 2001). In contrast, for individuals in whom no true cognitive change has occurred, change scores on individual cognitive tests would be both positive and negative, making their sum (i.e., the composite score) close to zero. However conclusions based on composite scores are limited to interpretation defined broadly by all tests in a battery, and don't allow consideration of performance changes on the specific measures of cognitive function from which the composite score is derived.

Apart from absolute difference scores and percentage change scores, statistical approaches to defining change (for single tests or composite scores) require some estimate of normal variability in performance over time. This normal variability is used to determine whether any change observed in the performance of the individual patient is meaningful (for a review, see Collie et al., 2002). Different change statistics derive this estimate of normal variability from different data sources. For example, some RCIs use the *SD* of difference scores as their denominator (Rasmussen et al., 2001). The RCI is considered the superior statistic for guiding decisions about change (Collie et al., 2002), although the clinician is faced with the problem of deciding upon the most appropriate control group. In most circumstances, this problem can be overcome by estimating the stability of performance from a matched control group, assessed on the same cognitive tests at the same test-retest intervals as the patient of interest. For ADHD however, the selection of a control group may be problematic because researchers contend that, in addition to subtle impairments in cognitive function, children with ADHD also show greater variability in performance than healthy, age-matched children without ADHD (Douglas, 1999). In fact, some argue that this increased variability is the cognitive hallmark of ADHD (Castellanos & Tannock, 2002), although the magnitude of this variability has not been quantified. If increased within-individual variability is part of the ADHD cognitive syndrome then the best estimate of normal variability in performance (in the absence of medication) would come from a group of children with ADHD who are assessed repeatedly while unmedicated. Thus, it is important to test the hypothesis that children with ADHD show greater variability in cognitive performance than that of age-matched children without ADHD. If the hypothesis is refuted, the stability data obtained from the group of healthy children would also provide an appropriate denominator to guide decisions about the significance of change in cognitive function in children with ADHD following medication.

The aim of the current study was to apply statistical decision rules to the cognitive test data of individual children with ADHD in order to classify whether each showed a cognitive response to medication. The ability of this technique to identify true treatment response was determined by the extent to which classifications of cognitive response were commensurate with classifications of behavioural response in the same children. Although there is some speculation that cognitive and behavioural responses to medication may be independent, previous published findings indicated that both cognitive and behavioural improvement occurred in the same ADHD group (Mehta et al., 2004; Pietrzak et al., 2006). Furthermore, behavioural response is the current standard by which medication response is determined, both clinically and in medication trials (Conners, 2002; Swanson et al., 1993). Therefore, behavioural response was used as a gold standard to determine the utility of the cognitive test and statistical rules in identifying treatment response. Before this analysis, we sought to determine whether the variability in cognitive performance in medication naïve children with ADHD was greater than that in age-, gender- and IQ-matched control children by computing estimates of test stability in the two groups and comparing them directly. To provide statistical power adequate to detect small differences in variability, we also compared the stability of performance in children with ADHD to that of a larger group of healthy children.

METHOD

Participants

The data were obtained from children who participated in two separate studies (Mollica et al., 2005; Mollica et al., submitted; refer to these papers for more detailed information about participants, materials and procedures). The first participant group included 87 healthy children aged between 8 and 12 years (42 males; $M = 120.10$ months, ±14.47). The remaining groups included 14 children with ADHD aged between 7 and 12 years (12 males, $M = 110.71$ months ±22.38) and 14 healthy children, each of whom was matched to a child with ADHD for gender and age (12 males, $M = 111.50$ months ±20.73; t (26) $= 0.10$, $p =.92$). The FSIQ of these two groups was also equivalent (healthy mean $= 104.43$, ±5.67; ADHD mean $= 100.07$, ±8.44; t (26)$= 1.60$, $p=.12$). Prior to enrolment in the study, all children with ADHD had met the DSM-IV symptom cut-off and impairment criteria for ADHD (combined type), as diagnosed by a child psychiatrist. The exclusion criteria for participants in the three groups have been described previously.

MEASURES

Behavioural Measures

The Child Behavior Checklist- parent form (CBCL; Achenbach, 1991) was completed for each participant prior to testing. The Rutter & Graham Interview Schedule was completed for each child during each testing session (Rutter & Graham, 1968), from which a composite Hyperactivity (RGIS-H) rating was calculated. In addition, the Abbreviated Conners Rating Scale (ACRS; Conners, 1985) and the Children's Impulsiveness Scale (CIS; Vance & Barnett, 2002) were completed within each testing session for the ADHD group and their matched controls. Total scores for the ACRS and CIS were used.

Cognitive Measures

The participants were repeatedly assessed using the CogState battery. This battery comprises seven tasks that assess psychomotor function (detection task), visual attention (identification, matching and monitoring tasks), executive function (working memory and sorting tasks) and memory (learning task). The dependent variable for the tests of psychomotor function and visual attention was mean reaction time (RT). Accuracy (i.e., the percentage of correct responses) was recorded for the tests of executive function and memory. These performance measures were used because they are the most appropriate for measuring cognitive change with children: they cause minimal practice effects, yield normal distributions, and allow enough variation in performance to detect decline and improvement in performance (Mollica et al., 2005). A description of the battery's administration and the seven cognitive tasks has been detailed previously.

PROCEDURE

The large group of healthy children was tested in groups of ten at their primary school. These children completed four administrations of the cognitive battery within a two-hour testing session, with 10-15 minute rest breaks in between administrations. In a separate study, the ADHD and matched control groups completed five administrations of the cognitive battery over three consecutive weekdays: two on day one, two on day two, and one on day three (see Table 1). Each testing session was completed within 30 minutes and participants had a two-hour break between sessions that were conducted on the same day. Immediately after completion of the first and third test sessions, the children with ADHD were administered a dose of stimulant medication. They received 2.5mg of dexamphetamine after session one and 7.5mg of dexamphetamine following session three (see Table 1; these doses are within the range of standard medication doses prescribed by the treating child psychiatrist). None of the matched control children were administered any medication throughout testing. Five children with ADHD were regularly taking stimulant medication prior to their involvement in the study: these children ceased taking their stimulant medication at least 24 hours prior to the first testing session and did not resume until the study was complete. Following each testing session, the assessor completed the RGIS for each child. In addition, the assessor completed the ACRS and CIS for each child in the ADHD group and their matched controls following each testing session.

Table 1. Schedule of testing for the participants with ADHD and their matched control group

	Session A	Two hour break	Session B
Day One	Assessment 1	2.5mg dexamphetamine	Assessment 2
Day Two	Assessment 3	7.5 mg dexamphetamine	Assessment 4
Day Three	Assessment 5		

Statistical Analysis

Treatment of Data from Cognitive Tasks and Behavioural Rating Scales
Each participant's CBCL ratings were converted to standardised T scores. The healthy children's T scores were inspected to ensure that none exceeded 65 (Achenbach, 1991). The RTs for each correct trial were identified and transformed using a logarithmic base 10 (log10) transformation to ensure that the data were suitable for parametric statistical analyses. The mean transformed RT for each individual was computed for the detection, identification, matching and monitoring tasks. For the working memory, sorting and learning tasks, the number of correct responses were recorded and expressed as a percentage of the total number of trials. Arcsine transformations were then applied to these percentage scores in order to normalise the data

distributions (Winer, 1971). Once complete, data analysis proceeded in two stages. The first compared variability in behaviour and cognitive function between the different groups to determine the most appropriate denominator for change equations. The second investigated the cognitive and behavioural change scores for each test within the ADHD group and the matched control group.

Stability of Cognitive Performance and Behavioural Ratings in ADHD

For each measure, performance on the initial baseline was excluded because a practice effects was identified previously in this data set, which reflected familiarisation from the first to second assessment (Mollica et al., 2005). In order to keep the experimental design balanced, behavioural data from the first assessment were also excluded for the ADHD participants and their matched controls. Data from the multiple baseline conditions was then submitted to a series of one-way Analysis of Variance (ANOVA) in order to determine the mean square residual (MSr) on each cognitive task (i.e., assessments two, three and four for the large healthy group, and assessments three and five for the ADHD and matched control groups). The square root of the MSr was then calculated to determine the within-subjects standard deviation (WSD; Bland & Altman, 1996) for each group on all of the cognitive measures. The WSD was also calculated using the behavioural ratings of the ADHD group and their matched controls. The F_{max} test statistic (Winer, 1971) was used to compare the magnitude of the estimates of variability for the behavioural measures between the ADHD group and their matched controls. For the WSD of the cognitive measures, two series of F_{max} tests were conducted: the ADHD group was compared to each of the groups of healthy children in separate analyses.

Defining Improvement on Cognitive and Behavioural Measures

The number of individuals in the control and ADHD groups who showed improvement under the low or high dose condition was computed for each behavioural and cognitive measure. For each individual, data from the two baseline assessments (i.e., assessments three and five) were collapsed to form a single, average baseline measure. Exploratory analysis indicated no difference between the baseline assessments for any cognitive or behavioural measure. Performance for the average baseline condition was then subtracted from performance for the low and high dose conditions, respectively. This difference was expressed as a ratio of the WSD to determine the treatment response ratio. For the cognitive and behavioural measures, ratios greater than

1.65 ($p <$ .05 one-tailed) were classified as a significant improvement. The number of individuals in the ADHD group showing improvement indicated the sensitivity of the test to stimulant medication. The false positive rate of the cut-off score was determined empirically by computing the number of individuals in the (untreated) control group who showed improvement on each behavioural and cognitive measure.

A response to treatment with stimulant medication might manifest as subtle improvement (i.e., less than the cut-off score) across a range of cognitive measures rather than as large improvement on two or more specific measures. Therefore, cognitive response was also classified using a *composite* score derived from change in performance on the seven cognitive performance measures (e.g., Rasmussen et al., 2001). This z-composite score was computed by summing the seven treatment response ratios for each individual in the ADHD and control groups for the low and high dose conditions. The *SD* of the z-composite score was computed from the control group and used as a denominator in the equation:

$$z\text{-composite score} = \frac{\text{individual's sum of treatment response ratios}}{SD \text{ of composite scores from the matched control group}}$$

Cognitive z-composite scores exceeding 1.65 ($p <$ .05 one-tailed) were used to classify general cognitive improvement. This method was also used to compute a z-composite score for the behavioural measures.

Definition of Cognitive and Behavioural Treatment Response in Individuals

The binomial probability tables of Ingraham and Aitken (1996) were used to determine the number of individuals that demonstrated significant improvement in cognitive or behavioural function following treatment with stimulant medication. For each individual, a cognitive treatment response was defined as a treatment response ratio of 1.65 or greater ($p <$ .05, one-tailed) on two or more of the seven cognitive measures. Given the smaller number of behavioural measures, the less conservative treatment response ratio of 1.50 or greater ($p <$ .05, one-tailed) on two or more measures was used to classify a behavioural treatment response. To check the model developed by Ingraham and Aitkin (1996) the same rules were applied to the behavioural ratings and cognitive performance of the non-ADHD, non-medicated control group. Any classification of treatment response in this group would be a false positive classification.

The possibility of an individual experiencing more subtle, but general improvement in function was investigated using the z-composite scores. For the cognitive *and* behavioural z-composite scores, treatment response was classified if the value exceeded 1.65 ($p < .05$ one-tailed). Therefore, to be classified as a cognitive responder an individual required a treatment response ratio of 1.65 or greater on two or more cognitive performance measures, a cognitive z-composite score of 1.65 or greater, or both. To be classified as a behavioural responder an individual required a treatment response ratio of 1.50 or greater on two or more behavioural rating scales, a behavioural z-composite score of 1.65 or greater, or both.

Validity of Cognitive Responder Classification

According to the criteria outlined above, each child could be classified into one of four response categories. These categories were: cognitive responder/behavioural responder (true positive classification), cognitive responder/behavioural non-responder (false positive classification), cognitive non-responder/behavioural responder (false negative classification) and cognitive non-responder/behavioural non-responder (true negative classification). The number of individuals within each of these classification categories was identified for both the low- and high-dose conditions separately. The association between the classification of cognitive and behavioural response was determined using the Chi-square test. The strength of the association between the magnitude of behavioural and cognitive response was then determined by calculating the Pearson's correlation coefficient (r) between the behavioural and cognitive z-composite scores at both the low- and high-dose conditions. Finally, the presence and strength of the association between the magnitude of cognitive response at the low- and high-dose conditions was examined by computing the Pearson's correlation coefficient between the cognitive z-composite score for both medication conditions. For all analyses, the alpha level used to indicate statistical significance was maintained at $p < .05$. This criterion was selected because this is a novel approach to investigating cognitive change in individual children, hence it was considered important to generate hypotheses for future investigation.

RESULTS

Stability of Cognitive Performance
and Behavioural Ratings in ADHD

The WSD for each cognitive measure in the two control groups and the ADHD group is shown in Table 2. The magnitude of the WSD was similar between the ADHD group and both control groups. In fact, no significant differences were found between the ADHD and control groups for the stability of performance on any cognitive measure. In contrast, behavioural measures were significantly more variable in the ADHD group than in the matched controls. Therefore, the groups' respective WSDs were used as the denominator for computation of standardised response magnitude scores for the cognitive and behavioural measures.

Table 2. A comparison of the within-subjects standard deviation (WSD) between a large sample of healthy control children (Control 1), a group of children with ADHD, and their matched control group (Control 2)

Measure	WSD			Fmax statistic	
	Control 1 ($n = 87$)	Control 2 ($n = 14$)	ADHD ($n = 14$)	Control 1 vs. ADHD	Control 2 vs. ADHD
Behavioural					
ACRS	-	0.57	1.94	-	11.58**
CIS	-	0.73	1.6	-	4.80*
RGIS-H	-	0.85	1.7	-	4.00*
Cognitive					
Detection (RT)	0.05	0.05	0.06	1.44	1.44
Identification (RT)	0.07	0.07	0.05	0.51	1.96
Matching (RT)	0.07	0.06	0.05	1.96	1.44
Monitoring (RT)	0.08	0.08	0.08	1.00	1.00
Working memory (Acc)	0.12	0.14	0.10	0.69	1.96
Sorting (Acc)	0.16	0.13	0.11	2.12	1.40
Learning (Acc)	0.11	0.13	0.11	1.00	1.40

Note. ACRS = Abbreviated Conners Rating Scale; CIS = Children's Impulsivity Scale; RGIS-H = Hyperactivity Composite score of the Rutter and Graham Interview Schedule; RT = reaction time; Acc = accuracy; * = $p < .05$; ** = $p < .01$.

Defining Treatment Response for Cognitive and Behavioural Measures

The number of individuals classified as showing improvement on each behavioural and cognitive measure in each group is shown in Table 3. Very few controls met the criteria for improvement on any behavioural measure. For the ADHD group, significantly more improvement was identified for the ACRS at the low- and high-dose and the CIS at the high-dose. However, the behavioural z-composite score showed the greatest amount of improvement in the ADHD group as well as yielding no false positive classifications.

For the cognitive performance measures, the number of individuals from the control group classified as showing improvement was uniformly low. The cognitive performance measures that were most sensitive to treatment response in children with ADHD were the detection task at both the low- and high-dose, and the identification and sorting tasks at the high-dose. Once again, the z-composite score was most sensitive to cognitive improvement following stimulant medication, as well as yielding no false positive classifications.

Defining Cognitive and Behavioural Treatment Response in Individuals

The number of individuals in each group whose improvement in behaviour ratings or cognitive performance was sufficient to be classified as a behavioural or cognitive treatment response is shown in Table 4. None of the control children was classified as either a behavioural or cognitive responder. In comparison, a significant proportion of the ADHD group met the criteria for classification as both behavioural (Chi-square = 6.09; $p < .05$) and cognitive (Chi-square = 4.67; $p = .05$) responders at the low-dose medication condition. Furthermore, this proportion more than doubled for both behavioural (Chi-square = 18.12; $p < .01$) and cognitive (Chi-square = 15.56; $p < .01$) responder classifications at the high-dose medication condition.

Table 3. Number of participants demonstrating
improvement on behavioural and cognitive measures

Measure	Group	Low-dose (Assessment two)	High-dose (Assessment four)
Behavioural			
ACRS	Healthy	0	0
	ADHD	7**	8**
CIS	Healthy	2	1
	ADHD	6	8**
RGIS-H	Healthy	1	2
	ADHD	2	3
z-composite	Healthy	0	0
	ADHD	3	11**
Cognitive			
Detection	Healthy	0	0
	ADHD	6**	7**
Identification	Healthy	0	0
	ADHD	3	4*
Matching	Healthy	1	2
	ADHD	3	5
Monitoring	Healthy	0	1
	ADHD	0	2
Working memory	Healthy	0	0
	ADHD	2	2
Sorting	Healthy	0	0
	ADHD	1	4*
Learning	Healthy	0	0
	ADHD	1	1
z-composite	Healthy	0	0
	ADHD	2	10**

Note. ACRS = Abbreviated Conners Rating Scale; CIS = Children's Impulsivity Scale; RGIS-H = Hyperactivity Composite score of the Rutter and Graham Interview Schedule; $* = p < .05$; $** = p < .01$.

Validity of Cognitive Responder Classification

Table 5 shows the association between the number of participants in each classification category within the ADHD group for the low- and high-dose medication conditions. No significant association was found between classifications of behavioural and cognitive response for the low-dose condition (Chi-square = 3.76; $p = .10$); however, the majority of cases in this analysis (57%) were classified as behavioural and cognitive non-responders. For the high-dose condition, there was a significant association between classification as a behavioural *and* cognitive responder (Chi-square = 9.55; p = .01) with the majority of cases (71%) classified as responders across both domains.

The magnitude of cognitive response observed in individual children with ADHD (as defined by the cognitive z-composite scores) was strongly associated with the magnitude of behavioural response in the same children (as defined by the behavioural z-composite score) for both the low- (r = .72; p < .01; see Figure 1) and high-dose conditions (r = .85; p < .01; see Figure 2). Finally, despite being too subtle to yield many cases of treatment response, the magnitude of cognitive response at the low-dose was associated significantly with the magnitude of cognitive response at the high-dose medication condition (r = .83; p < .01; see Figure 3) for the children with ADHD.

Table 4. Behaviour and cognitive responders for the ADHD group and their matched controls within each treatment condition

	Condition	
Group	Low-dose (assessment two)	High-dose (assessment four)
Behavioural measures		
Healthy	0	0
ADHD	5*	11**
Cognitive measures		
Healthy	0	0
ADHD	4*	10**

Note. * = p < .05; ** = p < .01.

Table 5. Summary of the number of children with ADHD in each classification category at both the low- and high-dose conditions

	Cognitive response	Cognitive non-response
Low-dose condition		
Behavioural response	3	2
Behavioural non-response	1	8
High-dose condition**		
Behavioural response	10	1
Behavioural non-response	0	3

Note. ** = p < .01.

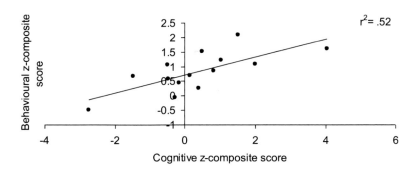

Figure 1. Scattergram of the z-composite scores for participants with ADHD in the low-dose condition.

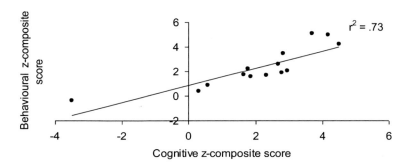

Figure 2. Scattergram of the z-composite scores for participants with ADHD in the high-dose condition.

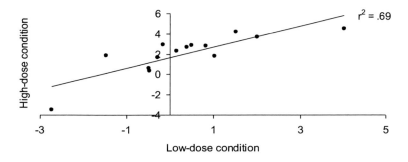

Figure 3. Scattergram of the cognitive z-composite scores for participants with ADHD at the low- and high-dose conditions.

DISCUSSION

The results of this study indicate that the statistical method developed for defining cognitive and behavioural response to stimulant medication was able to identify individuals with ADHD who showed a true positive response without classifying any treatment response in healthy, non-treated children assessed at the same time intervals. By considering simultaneously both the criterion used to define change on each cognitive or behavioural measure as well as the number of measures given, the decision rule yielded a high sensitivity and high specificity to treatment response. Although preliminary, these results suggest that it is possible to develop an evidence-based approach to clinical decision-making about the response to medication of individual children with ADHD. Whereas clinicians are experienced in making decisions about the effectiveness of medication on the basis of change in behavioural symptoms, the utility of cognitive function as a measure of treatment response in individual patients is not clear. By taking what has been learned about cognitive tests and statistical methods from other contexts (e.g., detecting cognitive decline after coronary surgery, concussion management; Collie et al., 2002) and modifying them so that they are appropriate for investigating ADHD, the current study provides a reliable method for identifying treatment response in individual children.

In the children with ADHD, the cognitive and behavioural response to medication (as defined in this study) was remarkably consistent following the high dose of medication. Ten participants (71%) were classified as having responded to the medication on both the behavioural rating scales and cognitive performance measures. Furthermore, the three children who showed no behavioural response also showed no cognitive response (see Table 5). The one inconsistent classification at the high dose occurred when a child who was classified as a behavioural responder did not satisfy the criteria for a cognitive response. However, inspection of the data for this case indicated that the child's cognitive composite score was actually 1.64; hence, she failed narrowly to satisfy the classification criterion for cognitive response (as shown in Figure 2). Thus, in contrast to the work of Sprague and Sleator (1977) the results of the current study suggest that a single dose of stimulant medication is effective in ameliorating behavioural *and* cognitive symptoms of ADHD.

Of the three children with ADHD who showed no behavioural or cognitive response at the high-dose, two also showed no improvement in cognitive and behavioural function at the low-dose of medication. Interestingly, the characteristics of these two non-responders were qualitatively similar to profiles of children with ADHD that are proposed to demonstrate a poor response to stimulant medication (for a review, see Gray & Kagan, 2000). For example, these two children had clinically significant ratings on the Anxious/Depressed subscale of the CBCL (i.e., scores of 75 and 76; M for responders = 57.75 ±4.90), as well as relatively low baseline ratings of behavioural disturbance on the ACRS (i.e., mean baseline ratings of 4 and 1.5; M for responders = 8.69 ±2.97). One of these children also had a co-morbid diagnosis of Generalised Anxiety Disorder. An increased severity of co-morbid internalizing symptoms such as anxiety and depression has been associated with a poor response to medication within both the cognitive and behavioural domains (DuPaul et al., 1994; Swanson et al., 1978; Tannock et al., 1995). In addition, children who display less severe behavioural symptoms of ADHD, including those measured by the Conners' rating scales (i.e., the ACRS), are less likely to demonstrate medication-related improvement (Buitelaar et al., 1995; Efron et al., 1997; Taylor et al., 1987). Therefore, the non-responsiveness of these two children is consistent with knowledge regarding variables that have been associated with poor response to stimulant medication in ADHD.

The third behavioural and cognitive non-responder at the high medication dose actually showed significant improvement in both cognitive and behavioural function following the low-dose. Although this finding is in contrast with the linear dose-response effects that are typically observed in ADHD (Greenhill, 2001), it also highlights the importance of considering inter-individual variation in medication response. For example, this may represent a case where treatment was optimised at a low-dose of stimulant medication. Previous studies have defined treatment response, albeit primarily based on behavioural symptoms, as occurring with improvement at *either* a low or high medication dose (e.g., Denney & Rapport, 1999). Had this same criterion been used in the current study, the number of true negatives would have been reduced to two and the number of true positive cognitive responders increased to 11 participants (79%).

When considered as a continuous variable, the magnitude of treatment response on the cognitive performance measures was associated in a strong, linear fashion with the magnitude of treatment response on the behavioural rating scales (see Figures 1 and 2). Furthermore, strong dose response relationships were evident in the linear association between cognitive response at the low and high doses (see Figure 3). These results highlight the internal consistency of the decision rules applied to define treatment response. Although factors that predict treatment response have not yet been elucidated

(Gray & Kagan, 2000), further investigation of possible predictor variables could occur using the current experimental design and cognitive assessment methodology in a larger sample.

It is important to emphasise that the ability of the current methodology to identify treatment response in children with ADHD is not due only to the statistical criteria applied. The ability of the current study to detect cognitive change was based on a number of important methodological and statistical issues that were considered simultaneously in this study. For example, the performance measures to which the statistical rules were applied were selected because they yielded data that were normally distributed, did not suffer from floor or ceiling effects, and were not subject to range restriction (Mollica et al., 2005; Silbert et al., 2004). Furthermore, these performance measures were generated by a series of cognitive tasks that minimise the effects of practice, could be administered rapidly, and could be performed reliably by healthy children and children with ADHD (Mollica et al., 2005; Mollica et al., submitted). A study of groups of children has also indicated that the psychomotor function, attention, executive function and memory tasks were sensitive to both ADHD (when compared to healthy children) and the effect of stimulant medication (Mollica, et al., submitted). Finally, the current experimental design was developed to allow assessment of the effects of medication in children with ADHD without substantially disrupting clinical practice or requiring that medication be withheld for a substantial period of time. Thus, the development of the statistical approach used here could occur only after the foundations for data generation had been completed. Now that the methodology has been developed, it needs to be validated in other clinical settings using additional types of single-case investigations (e.g., Kent et al., 1999).

Although the current study was designed to identify cognitive change in individual children, the results are also relevant to aetiological models of ADHD. For example, it was surprising to find that the stability of cognitive performance was equivalent in unmedicated children with ADHD and healthy matched controls (see Table 2). There appears to be general consensus in the literature that the cognitive performance of individual children with ADHD is subject to greater variability than in children without the disorder (Douglas, 1999). This variability is detected most reliably on simple stimulus response tasks, and in fact some tasks deliberately entail long administration times to accentuate inconsistent performance within a single assessment session. The reason for this variability in performance is not understood completely. For example, it is reasonable to expect that children whose disorder is characterised by a difficulty in sitting still and remaining 'on task' show unreliable performance on cognitive tasks that are long, repetitive, and simple. Alternatively, the variability in performance could reflect true central nervous system disruption. Recent reviews by Castellanos, Tannock, and colleagues have lead to the hypothesis of a brain-behaviour model that links the performance variability shown by children with ADHD on clinical instruments to disordered temporal processing related to cerebellar dysfunction (see Castellanos & Tannock, 2002; Paule et al., 2000).

In our research involving children and adults with different psychiatric disorders, we have employed brief testing sessions in order to maximise compliance and thereby attain data with the greatest reliability (e.g., Cairney et al., 2001; Maruff et al., 1996; Wood et al., 1999). Consequently, the cognitive tasks used here were designed to keep administration time under 20 minutes. Therefore, in the ADHD group, the normal performance stability at baseline may have occurred because these children were not assessed for long enough, or, because seven different tasks were given within the 20 minute assessment, the duration of each task may have been too brief. Nevertheless, the current results suggest that short administration times did not decrease the sensitivity of the tasks to dysfunctions associated with ADHD. Moreover, these cognitive tasks provide reliable data with attractive statistical properties of normality and homogeneity of variance, which allow them to be investigated using the more powerful parametric statistical techniques.

The data set used here to explore the classification of treatment response in individuals has been previously employed to study medication-related improvement in cognitive function at a group level in ADHD (Mollica et al., submitted). In this previous study, the ADHD group showed significant improvement in performance on the detection, identification, monitoring and learning tasks following the high-dose of stimulant medication. It may have been expected that these tasks would also possess the greatest sensitivity to medication-related improvement in individual children with ADHD. This was not the case, as the tasks for which the greatest number of significant responses occurred were the detection, identification, matching and sorting tasks (see Table 3).

Interestingly, the cognitive composite score provided the greatest sensitivity to treatment response at both the low- and high-dose, while yielding no false positive classifications. In addition, the magnitude of response to treatment as defined by this cognitive composite score was correlated strongly between the low- and high-dose medication conditions. Although preliminary, these data suggests that response to stimulant medication may be characterised by subtle and generalised cognitive improvement rather than as a large improvement in specific aspects of cognitive function. These data are consistent with previous conclusions (Bergman et al., 1991) and highlight the heterogeneous nature of individual medication-response in ADHD. They also show how the performance of individual children with ADHD can be analysed in group studies of ADHD, at least in the form of post-hoc analyses. The statistical methods presented here would be appropriate for such analyses provided that the tests used to assess cognitive function possess the desired metric properties (as discussed above and in Mollica et al., 2005).

The findings of the current study are preliminary, and replication is warranted to address several limitations of this design. First, participants within the ADHD group were recruited from a Child and Adolescent Mental Heath Service and included children who required on-going case management. Consequently, these children were more likely to experience an increased rate of symptom severity and co-morbid difficulties. These clinical features may have influenced the participant's cognitive performance as well as their response to stimulant medication. In addition, these children were all diagnosed with ADHD-CT. Given the known differences in cognitive dysfunction across ADHD subtypes (Nigg et al., 2002), replication of this study using participants with primarily inattentive and hyperactive/impulsive subtypes would be of importance prior to clinical application of the methods described herein. Second, replication with a larger sample is warranted to add support to the inferences outlined above. Although clear trends in medication response were observed at the high-dose condition, it is of importance to validate these and the more general findings by using a larger group of participants and increasing the statistical power of analyses. In addition, the behavioural measures were specifically designed to be readministered at such brief intervals; the reliability and validity of these measures when used in this manner could be clarified with additional research. Finally, it may be useful to investigate the application of these cognitive assessment tasks and statistical methodologies across greater test-retest intervals. Although this brief medication trial was practical in minimising disruption to clinical management, increasing the time between assessments could be useful in aiding investigation into more long-term medication effects and potential side-effects. As outlined in a previous study, the integration of double-blind methodology is also important for future investigations to prevent the effects of experimenter bias or participant placebo effects (see Mollica et al., submitted). Overall, however, the statistical method explored within the current study appears to be a novel and effective way of empirically investigating the effects of stimulant medication on the cognitive and behavioural function of individual children with ADHD.

The next study will outline a novel "intensive design" method for assessing stimulant medication-related improvement in cognitive function in children with ADHD.

Chapter 2

STUDY 2

Stimulant medication is currently the most effective pharmacological treatment for ADHD, although medication-responsiveness can vary according to many factors such as the severity of ADHD symptoms, medication dose, or the presence of co-morbid disorders (DuPaul et al. 1994; Buitelaar et al. 1995; Denney & Rapport 1999). The rate of true non-response is less than 25% (Elia et al. 1991; Santosh & Taylor 2000; Clarke et al. 2002).

In addition to the core symptoms of ADHD, impairment in cognitive function is reliably observed in ADHD and is an important aspect of the clinical presentation of this disorder (Denney & Rapport 2001; Castellanos & Tannock 2002). Further, improvement in cognitive function remains an important end point in studies assessing the effectiveness of novel and established therapies for ADHD (Gittelman-Klien & Klein 1975, 1976). Recent open-label and placebo-controlled trials demonstrate that stimulant medication improves cognitive function (de Sonneville et al. 1994; Efron et al. 1997; Bedard et al. 2003), although the majority of these studies base such conclusions on observations of improved performance on measures of speeded reaction time or inhibition. Although these improvements are reliable, their magnitude is generally moderate (an average effect size of 0.6) and less than the magnitude of improvement in ADHD symptoms (Greenhill 2001; Conners 2002). A small number of studies have measured the effect of stimulant medication on higher-level cognitive functions such as executive function or memory in prospective studies and reported equivocal results (Gittelman-Klien & Klein 1975, 1976; Tannock & Schachar 1992; Aman et al. 1998; Scheres et al. 2003). For example, some find no stimulant medication-related improvement in higher cognitive functions (Gittelman-Klien and Klein 1975;

Scheres et al. 2003), or where improvement is detected, the magnitude is small (effect sizes <0.5; Gittelman-Klien & Klein 1976; Brodeur & Pond 2001).

There are a number of explanations for the different effects of stimulant medication observed across different cognitive functions. First, stimulant medication may exert greater effects on the simple cognitive functions required for tests such as the CPT, stop, and vigilance tasks compared to the more complex and multifactorial cognitive functions required for performance on executive function and memory tasks. Consequently, complex cognitive functions may require higher doses of medication to yield improvements of the same magnitude as that found for simple cognitive tasks (Swanson et al. 1991). Third, simple attention and motor tasks may be more sensitive to the measurement of cognitive change than tests of higher cognitive functions because these tests generally deliver more observations or trials per assessment, yield interval level data (e.g., reaction time) that are not constrained by floor or ceiling effects, and are less susceptible to the effects of practice than tests of higher cognitive function. For example, tasks such as the Wisconsin Card Sorting Task (WCST) and Tower of London (TOL) are commonly employed in ADHD research, yet they often yield restricted ranges of possible scores and may induce large practice effects when given repeatedly. These factors can reduce the sensitivity of such tests to subtle cognitive change (Basso et al. 1999; Collie et al. 2003). Finally, poor study designs can impede the detection of change. For example, inadequate control for the effects of repeated assessment, such as that found with natural history studies or studies without a crossover design, can produce data sets that obscure true change in cognitive function and promote erroneous inferences (McCaffrey & Westervelt 1995). Thus, to measure simultaneously the magnitude of stimulant medication-related improvement on tasks requiring either simple or complex cognitive functions, and to compare this to the magnitude of improvement in symptoms, it is necessary to control practice effects and to utilise tests that yield data that are optimal for the statistical analysis of change.

We have recently modified a series of tests of psychomotor, attentional, executive and memory function so that they can be given rapidly and repeatedly, do not give rise to practice effects once individuals are familiar with the task requirements, and generate optimal data for the assessment of change. These tests can be performed easily by children and are sensitive to cognitive changes associated with head injury, and fatigue and alcohol intoxication in adults (Mollica et al. 2005; Falleti et al. 2003). Therefore, these cognitive tests may be also useful for assessing stimulant-related cognitive change in children with ADHD.

Two experimental designs are typically used to study the effects of stimulant medication on cognitive function in ADHD: open-label and placebo controlled trials. In open-label trials, the participants, their parents and the assessors are aware of medication status, which can potentially influence performance or ratings. Also, the effect of repeated assessment cannot be determined because there is generally no appropriate unmedicated control group. Double-blind, placebo-controlled crossover trial designs are now common in ADHD research and this methodology does control the effects of expectancy and practice. However, such trials are expensive and require that children with ADHD have their medication withheld for a substantial period of time in order to complete the placebo condition (de Sonneville et al. 1994). The withholding of medication or disruption to children's conventional clinical management may be warranted when there is good *prima face* evidence for medication efficacy and broader clinical trials are required for regulatory approval. However, hypothesis-generating studies about the relationship between cognitive functions, symptoms, medication and the disorder may not warrant such disruption or expense. Given that the half-life of stimulant medication is generally short, it is possible to design a study in which practice effects are controlled, children are assessed on and off their medication at brief retest intervals, and reliable conclusions about the effect of medication on cognitive function can be made. Children with ADHD can act as their own controls by being assessed before and after taking medication on the same day (AB design). Repeating the cognitive assessments each day while the children are unmedicated, and also at the end of the trial, provides an estimate of any practice effects that may have arisen from the repeated assessment (ABA design). Furthermore, different doses of stimulant medication can be given on different days to determine whether dose-response relationships exist for any of the cognitive functions measured (ABACA design). Provided the assessments are brief, children and their parents are not inconvenienced and there will be minimal disruption to the child's conventional clinical management (Mollica et al. 2004). Uhlenhuth et al. (1977) and Klein (2008) strongly support such "intensive designs" to determine whether a given child is actually responding to a particular treatment.

The aim of the current study is to investigate the effect of low and high doses of stimulant medication on psychomotor, attentional, executive and memory function and compare this to the effect on symptoms in children with

ADHD assessed using an ABACA experimental design. The null hypothesis is that there would be no differences in performance between the baseline and the low- or high-dose medication conditions in the ADHD group.

METHOD

Participants

The participants included a clinical group of 14 children with ADHD [12 males; 110.71 (22.38) months; full scale IQ 100.07 (8.44)] and a group of healthy children matched to the ADHD group for gender, age and full scale IQ [12 males; 111.50 (20.73); t (26) = 0.10, p=.92; full scale IQ 104.43 (5.67); t (26) = 1.60, p=.12]. All children with ADHD met DSM-IV criteria for ADHD, combined type (ADHD-CT), defined by a semi-structured clinical interview with the child's parent(s) [Anxiety Disorders Interview Schedule for Children (A-DISC) (Silverman & Albano 1996)] and a parent and/or teacher report assessing the core symptom domains of ADHD-CT being greater than 1.5 standard deviations above the mean for a given child's age and gender [Abbreviated Conners' Rating Scale (ACRS) score 21.48 (4.73) (Conners 1997)]. The children were all medication naïve and met the inclusion criteria of living in a family home (and not in an institution) and attending normal primary schools. Exclusion criteria for the ADHD group included: colour blindness, hearing impairment, a history of major neurological impairment, or a Full Scale Intelligence Quotient (FSIQ) below 80. Five participants had co-morbid psychiatric diagnoses (oppositional defiant disorder n = 3, generalised anxiety disorder n = 2).

Healthy control participants were recruited from a primary school and selected to match each ADHD participant for age, gender and full scale IQ. Exclusion criteria for the healthy participants included: colour blindness; hearing impairment; past or present psychiatric or neurological disorder; an estimated FSIQ below 80; or a T score of 60 or greater on any subscale of the *Child Behaviour Checklist-* Parent and Teacher Form (CBCL; Achenbach, 1991). No child in the healthy group received any medication during the study. No child withdrew or was excluded from the study. The study was approved by institutional ethics committees, and all children and their parents gave informed consent before beginning the study.

Measures

Intelligence Testing
All of the children with ADHD completed the Wechsler Intelligence Scale for Children-Fourth Edition (WISC-IV) (Wechsler, 2004).

Clinical Measures
The CBCL attention subscale T score was used to compare the participant groups. The ACRS was used to rate the children's behaviour within each testing session (approximately 30 minutes duration). The Children's Impulsiveness Scale (CIS; Vance & Barnett 2002) comprises 10 items that list and describe common features of behavioural impulsivity. The assessor is required to indicate the frequency of these behaviours as displayed by each child according to a four-point scale ranging from zero (*absence*) to three (*continuous*). The total CIS score was analysed in the present study. The *Revised Children's Manifest Anxiety Scale* (RCMAS; Reynolds & Richmond 1978) was used to gain subjective reports of anxiety. The total RCMAS score was analysed in the present study. The *Rutter & Graham Interview Schedule* (Rutter & Graham 1968) was employed to provide information about symptoms of anxiety and hyperactivity. Composite anxiety (RGIS-A) and hyperactivity (RGIS-H) ratings were analysed in the present study.

Cognitive Measures
The cognitive assessment battery was presented on lap top computers complete with headphones. All tasks within the battery were adaptations of standard neuropsychological and experimental psychological tests, and assess a range of cognitive functions such as psychomotor speed, attention, decision-making and working memory. This battery required approximately 15-20 minutes to complete. It consisted of seven tasks in the form of card games that were presented in succession on a green background. In order to aid individuals with the task, written instructions were presented to the left of the screen to indicate the rule for each new task. Participants were then given an interactive demonstration and, once they had successfully completed a sufficient number of practice trials to demonstrate their awareness of the rules, the task began.

A grey keyboard resembling a computer keyboard appeared in the lower half of the computer screen and the cards associated with each task were presented in the upper half. Participants were only required to respond with two keys throughout the entire battery by using the 'D' or 'K' keys. The beginning of each new task was indicated with a shuffling of the cards. An error beep sounded when an individual pressed an incorrect key at any time. Each trial was time limited and the same error beep sounded if a response was not made within the required time. Participants were able to pause the test at any stage using the 'Escape' key. The dependent variables recorded for each task included reaction time (RT) and accuracy (i.e., the percentage of correct responses). The seven tasks included in the battery have been described previously (Faletti et al. 2003).

Procedure

A parent/guardian for each child completed the CBCL prior to testing. Each participant completed five testing sessions over three consecutive weekdays at 1000 hours and 1300 hours: two on day one, two on day two, and one on day three. Each testing session was completed within 30 minutes and participants had a two-hour break between sessions that were conducted on the same day. During this break, the children with ADHD had free time with a parent/guardian in a waiting room with a play area. The healthy children were tested at their primary school and participated in regular school activities between same-day testing sessions.

The children were tested individually in a small, quiet room. At the beginning of each session participants completed the RCMAS independently. Next, children were seated at a computer and instructed to position their headphones. They were informed that instructions for each task would appear to the left of the screen and that they were required to complete each task as quickly and as accurately as possible. They were also told that an error beep would sound each time they made a mistake and that they could briefly pause the test if needed. The experimenter was seated next to participants throughout each trial and remained silent once the administration had begun. The children were informed that the experimenter was unable to provide assistance with the task itself; however, assistance was provided if a child demonstrated difficulty in reading or comprehending the task instructions. Following completion of the computerised task, the experimenter completed the ACRS, CIS and the RGIS for each child based on his or her behaviour during the entire testing session.

Immediately after completion of the first and third sessions, the children with ADHD were administered a dosage of stimulant medication. They received 2.5mg of Dexamphetamine after session one and 7.5mg of

Dexamphetamine following session three. The healthy children were not administered any medication throughout testing.

Statistical Analysis

Each participant's CBCL ratings were converted to standardised T scores. The healthy children's T scores were inspected to ensure that none exceeded 60. For each of the cognitive measures the number of correct responses was recorded and expressed as a percentage of the total trials. Arcsine transformations were then applied to these percentage scores in order to normalise the distributions of data in each group (Hopkins 2008). The reaction times (RTs) for each correct trial were identified and transformed using a log10 transformation. The mean log10 RT for each individual was computed for each test.

For each measure, performance on the initial baseline was excluded because it is known that familiarisation can occur from the first to second assessment in healthy children (Mollica et al. 2005). In order to keep the experimental design balanced, clinical data from the first assessment was also excluded. Data for the remaining two baseline assessments (assessments three and five) were then collapsed to form a single average baseline measure for each dependent variable. Exploratory analysis had indicated no difference between the baseline assessments for any cognitive measure.

Cognitive performance and clinical ratings were compared between-groups only for the average baseline condition, as both groups were not medicated at the time of assessments two and four. For each statistically significant between-group difference, the magnitude of that difference was calculated using an estimate of effect size (Cohen's d; Cohen 1988).

The main hypotheses in the study were tested by the presence of differences in performance between the baseline and the low- or high-dose medication conditions in the ADHD group. These were tested statistically by setting two orthogonal t-tests (average baseline versus low-dose medication condition, and average baseline versus high-dose medication condition) within a repeated measures analysis of variance (ANOVA). Inspection of any change in performance over the same assessment schedule in children without ADHD (using identical analyses) allowed us to determine the effect of repeated cognitive assessment independent of the state of disorder or medication. The magnitude of significant within-group differences was computed using a repeated measures effect size estimate (Dunlap's d; Dunlap et al. 1996). Data from the two groups were not compared directly in an ANOVA because this would have lead to an unbalanced design with medication status and group confounded.

Despite the relatively large number of statistical tests conducted in this study, the alpha level used to indicate statistical significance was maintained at $p \leq .05$. That criterion was selected because this is a relatively new approach to understanding the effects of medication on cognitive function and should therefore err toward generating hypotheses for future research. However, theoretical inferences were protected from false positive results because, even though many measures were used in the study, any change detected in the different cognitive and clinical measures following medication in the ADHD group was by definition correlated. In addition, by considering both the statistical significance and effect size of each comparison it was possible to identify any significant but meaningless differences ($d < 0.2$).

RESULTS

Between-Group Comparison on the Average Baseline Condition

Group means for the clinical and cognitive measures on the average baseline condition are displayed in Table 1, together with the results of t-tests and an estimate of effect sizes. The ADHD group received significantly higher ratings for all of the clinical measures of ADHD-related symptomatology. The magnitude of the group differences was large on each of these measures ($d = 2.40$ to 4.60). The groups did not differ on subjective or objective measures of anxiety. For measures of cognitive function, the performance speed of the ADHD group was significantly slower on the detection, identification and simple matching tasks with these group differences being large in magnitude ($ds > 1.00$).

Within-Group Analysis of Change on Clinical and Cognitive Measures

Group means for the clinical measures at each assessment are displayed in Table 2. A summary of the results of the t-tests used to compare performance between assessments and estimates of effect sizes are shown in Table 3. For the healthy children, no differences were observed between average baseline and the second or fourth assessments on any clinical measure. For the ADHD group, a significant reduction in symptom severity from the average baseline was found on the ACRS, CIS and RGIS-H. On each of these measures, the magnitude of symptom reduction from baseline to the high-dose condition was substantially greater than that observed for the low-dose condition. Figure 1 illustrates effect sizes for the change in the clinical measures of both groups across assessment conditions.

Table 1. Between-group comparison of clinical and cognitive measures at baseline

Measures	Group	M	SD	$t(26)$	d
ACRS	healthy	1.89	1.42	-6.29**	2.58
	ADHD	8.18	3.46		
CIS	healthy	2.93	1.43	-6.18**	2.40
	ADHD	7.43	2.32		
RGIS-H	healthy	2.46	0.82	-6.21**	2.47
	ADHD	5.46	1.61		
RGIS-A	healthy	0.00	0.00	-1.79	0.96
	ADHD	0.18	0.37		
CMAS	healthy	7.89	4.36	-1.19	0.46
	ADHD	10.57	7.22		
CBCL- Att	healthy	52.64	3.52	-11.92**	4.60
	ADHD	73.07	5.36		
Cognitive					
Detection	healthy	2.54	0.08	-3.94**	1.52
	ADHD	2.69	0.11		
Identification	healthy	2.80	0.09	-2.63**	1.01
	ADHD	2.91	0.12		
Simple matching	healthy	2.91	0.09	-3.56**	1.36
	ADHD	3.04	0.11		
Monitoring	healthy	2.63	0.09	-0.64	0.24
	ADHD	2.66	0.12		
Working memory	healthy	1.30	0.12	0.46	0.18
	ADHD	1.27	0.22		
Complex matching	healthy	1.25	0.20	1.40	0.53
	ADHD	1.14	0.23		
Learning	healthy	1.03	0.12	1.33	0.50
	ADHD	0.97	0.12		

Note. ACRS = Abbreviated Conners Rating Scale; CIS = Children's Impulsivity Scale; RGIS-H = Rutter and Graham Interviewing Schedule- Hyperactivity score; RGIS-A = Rutter and Graham Interviewing Schedule- Anxiety score; CMAS = Children's Manifest Anxiety Scale; ** indicates significant improvement from baseline, p < .01.

Table 2. Group means (SD) for the clinical and cognitive measures, within-group comparison across conditions and r^2 values for the linear trendline equation

Measures	Group	Average baseline	Assessment 2 (low dose)	Assessment 4 (high dose)	r^2
Clinical					
ACRS	healthy	1.89 (1.42)	2.21 (1.93)	1.93 (1.44)	
	ADHD	8.18 (3.46)	4.86 (2.51)**	3.79 (1.63)**	0.92
CIS	healthy	2.93 (1.43)	2.50 (1.34)	3.00 (1.30)	
	ADHD	7.43 (2.32)	5.71 (2.55)**	4.64 (1.91)**	0.98
RGIS-H	healthy	2.46 (0.82)	2.71 (1.33)	2.64 (1.01)	
	ADHD	5.46 (1.61)	4.36 (1.78)**	3.21 (1.37)**	0.99
RGIS-A	healthy	0.00	0.00	0.00	
	ADHD	0.18 (0.37)	0.21 (0.43)	0.07 (0.27)	0.65
RCMAS	healthy	7.89 (4.36)	7.79 (3.79)	7.57 (4.01)	
	ADHD	10.57 (7.22)	12.00 (8.05)	10.64 (7.07)	0.01
Cognitive					
Detection	healthy	2.54 (0.08)	2.56 (0.06)	2.55 (0.07)	
	ADHD	2.69 (0.11)	2.60 (0.08)**	2.57 (0.07)**	0.92
Measures	Group	Average baseline	Assessment 2 (low dose)	Assessment 4 (high dose)	r^2
Identification	healthy	2.80 (0.09)	2.81 (0.06)	2.84 (0.09)	
	ADHD	2.91 (0.12)	2.87 (0.14)	2.86 (0.14)*	0.89
Simple matching	healthy	2.91 (0.09)	2.90 (0.09)	2.93 (0.10)	
	ADHD	3.04 (0.11)	3.03 (0.11)	3.00 (0.12)	0.92
Monitoring	healthy	2.63 (0.09)	2.67 (0.12)	2.67 (0.08)	
	ADHD	2.66 (0.12)	2.67 (0.17)	2.60 (0.11)**	0.63
Working memory	healthy	1.30 (0.12)	1.27 (0.18)	1.25 (0.15)	
	ADHD	1.27 (0.22)	1.18 (0.21)	1.28 (0.18)	0.01
Complex matching	healthy	1.25 (0.20)	1.15 (0.23)#	1.20 (0.18)#	
	ADHD	1.14 (0.23)	1.05 (0.17)	1.17 (0.18)	0.06
Learning	healthy	1.03 (0.12)	0.97 (0.11)##	1.01 (0.16)	
	ADHD	0.97 (0.12)	0.97 (0.16)	1.03 (0.14)*	0.75

Note. ACRS = Abbreviated Conners Rating Scale; CIS = Children's Impulsivity Scale; RGIS-H = Rutter and Graham Interviewing Schedule- Hyperactivity score; RGIS-A = Rutter and Graham Interviewing Schedule- Anxiety score; CMAS = Children's Manifest Anxiety Scale; ** indicates significant improvement from baseline, p < .01; * indicates significant improvement from baseline, p < .05; ## indicates significant decline from baseline, p < .01; # indicates significant decline from baseline, p < .05.

**Table 3. t-statistics and effects size estimates of the change in
clinical and cognitive measures across assessment conditions
within the healthy and ADHD groups**

Measure	Group	Baseline v low		Baseline v high	
		t	d	t	d
Clinical					
ACRS	healthy	-0.87	0.18	-0.43	0.02
	ADHD	4.28**	1.06	5.12**	1.52
CIS	healthy	-0.96	0.31	0.35	-0.05
	ADHD	3.78**	0.70	4.63**	1.30
RGIS-H	healthy	0.80	-0.22	0.75	-0.19
	ADHD	3.08**	0.65	7.87**	1.48
RGIS-A	healthy	-	-	-	-
	ADHD	0.43	-0.09	-1.38	0.32
CMAS	healthy	-0.26	0.02	-0.82	0.07
	ADHD	1.57	-0.18	0.13	-0.01
Cognitive					
Detection	healthy	0.96	-0.20	0.49	-0.06
	ADHD	-4.27**	0.90	-5.82**	1.07
Identification	healthy	0.49	-0.11	1.61	-0.36
	ADHD	-1.39	0.33	-2.37*	0.41
Simple matching	healthy	-0.60	0.12	1.02	-0.25
	ADHD	-0.92	0.14	-1.51	0.33
Monitoring	healthy	1.53	-0.32	1.84	-0.43
	ADHD	0.37	-0.05	-3.08**	0.54
Working memory	healthy	0.90	-0.25	1.35	-0.40
	ADHD	1.78	-0.45	-0.13	0.04
Complex matching	healthy	2.27#	-0.47	2.11#	-0.31
	ADHD	-1.86	0.43	-0.63	0.17
Learning	healthy	2.98##	-0.50	0.53	-0.14
	ADHD	-0.17	0.03	-2.47*	0.45

Note. ACRS = Abbreviated Conners Rating Scale; CIS = Children's Impulsivity Scale;
RGIS-H = Rutter and Graham Interviewing Schedule- Hyperactivity score; RGIS-
A = Rutter and Graham Interviewing Schedule- Anxiety score; CMAS =
Children's Manifest Anxiety Scale; ** indicates significant improvement from
baseline, p < .01; * indicates significant improvement from baseline, p < .05; ##
indicates significant decline from baseline, p < .01; # indicates significant decline
from baseline, p < .05.

Group mean performance on each of the cognitive measures is shown in
Table 2. A summary of the results of the t-tests used to compare performance
between assessments and estimates of effect size are shown in Table 3. For the
healthy children, no change in cognitive performance was identified between
the average baseline and the second or fourth assessments. A significant

decline in performance accuracy was observed for the second and fourth assessments on the complex matching task and the second assessment on the learning task. The magnitude of these performance declines was low to moderate according to convention (d = -0.13 to -0.49; Cohen 1988). For the ADHD group, a significant improvement in performance on the detection task was observed from the average baseline to the low-dose *and* high-dose medication conditions. The magnitude of this improvement was greater for the high-dose condition (see Table 3). Improvements from the average baseline to the high-dose medication condition were also observed for performance speed on the identification and monitoring tasks, and performance accuracy on the learning task. The magnitude of improvements in performance for the ADHD group ranged from moderate to high (d = 0.41 to 1.04). Figure 1 displays the effect sizes of performance change on the cognitive measures for both groups across assessment conditions.

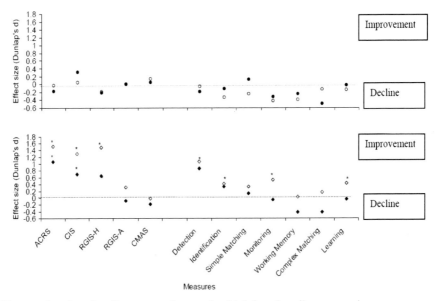

Note. • =lowdose-baseline comparison and ○=highdose-baseline comparison;
* = significant improvement in comparison to the average baseline condition.

Figure 1. Changes in the clinical and cognitive measures across conditions for the healthy (upper) and ADHD (lower) groups, as estimated by effect size.

DISCUSSION

The results of the study indicate that a novel within-subjects design can be used to examine the short-term effects of stimulant medication on cognitive and behavioural functions in children with ADHD, without substantially altering their clinical management. First, as expected, children with ADHD showed high levels of disordered behaviour when unmedicated, although self-reported and objective ratings of anxiety were within normal range. With medication, the levels of ADHD symptoms and hyperactive behaviour were reduced in a dose-dependent fashion. When considered against the conventions for determining experimental effect sizes, the magnitude of improvement with the highest dose was large (Cohen, 1988). Despite this reduction however, there was still overlap between distributions of pre- and post-medication symptom ratings. Thus, stimulant medication did not ameliorate symptoms completely in children with ADHD, even at high doses.

Interestingly, the unmedicated children with ADHD performed worse than age-, IQ-, and gender-matched controls only in the speed of psychomotor function (detection task) and the speed of visual attentional functions (identification and simple matching tasks). The magnitude of these impairments ranged from moderate to large. Following the low dose of stimulant medication, performance improved significantly only in the speed of psychomotor function (detection task). However at the higher dose, improvements were observed in the speed of psychomotor function (detection task), visual attention (identification and monitoring) and in the accuracy of learning. Although the magnitude of these medication-related improvements was moderate to large, it was more subtle than that observed for the response of behavioural symptoms to stimulant medication in the same children (Figure 1).

The larger effect of stimulant medication on ADHD symptoms relative to cognitive function has been reported previously and described in research reviews; yet there is currently no explanation for this difference (Greenhill 2001; Conners 2002). It is possible that the cognitive sequelae of ADHD are more complex than the characteristic behavioural symptoms and are therefore more treatment resistant. Alternatively, the cognitive dysfunctions may be comparatively less severe than the behavioural problems, thus the magnitude of improvement required to normalise cognitive function is substantially less. The results of the current study support the latter proposal. First, the magnitude of group differences at baseline was substantially greater for the behavioural measures (see Table 1). In addition, observation of the means in

Table 2 shows that during the high-dose medication condition, the ADHD group was comparable to the healthy group across most cognitive measures (Cohen's $d < 0.30$ for the detection, identification, working memory, complex matching and learning tasks) but not those of clinical function. Thus, the larger effect of stimulant medication on behavioural symptoms compared to cognitive function in children with ADHD may simply reflect a greater degree of dysfunction within the behavioural domain.

Although the interrelationships between cognitive function, behavioural symptoms and stimulant medication are central to current neurobiological theories of ADHD, surprisingly few studies have investigated these factors concurrently using a prospective design. Where these studies have been conducted, the results have varied between them. Some variation in research findings may reflect methodological differences, such as the types of tests used, the sample sizes studied, inclusion/exclusion criteria for ADHD, or the time period over which pre and post-medication assessment occurred. Despite this variability, there is consistent evidence that the speed of performance is improved following stimulant medication on relatively simple speeded response tasks (vigilance and reaction time tasks). This also occurred in the current study, where performance improved on the psychomotor and visual attention tasks following medication. Unfortunately, as few studies have reported the medication-related effect sizes (or provided statistics sufficient for their post-hoc calculation) it is not possible to determine whether the magnitude of improvement differs between experimental conditions. Alternatively, some studies report that the magnitude of improvement in performance on simple speeded psychomotor or visual attentional tasks shows a linear response relationship with the dose of stimulant medication (Barkley et al. 1991; O'Toole et al. 1997). Although within the current study improvements over baseline at the low and high medication dose were observed only on the measure of psychomotor function, linear trends were fitted to the mean cognitive performance of the ADHD group across the baseline, low and high dose conditions. These trends were significant for the detection, identification and simple matching tasks, with the variance in performance explained by medication approximately 90% for each task. Thus, robust dose response relationships were also detected. Medication was also found to facilitate performance accuracy on the learning task within the present study. Again, a significant linear trend was observed with approximately 75% of the variance in performance explained by medication dose. Similarly, other studies have reported improvement in memory and learning with low to moderate doses of stimulant medication in children with

ADHD (Sprague and Sleator 1977; Evans et al.1986; Barkley et al. 1989). This consistency of outcome on learning task performance is also provocative, as memory impairment is not generally considered within current cognitive neuroscience models of ADHD.

Cross-sectional studies of cognitive function in ADHD consistently find impairment in executive function (for a review, see Pennington and Ozonoff, 1996; Kempton et al., 1999; Barnett et al., 2001, 2005; Shallice et al., 2002; Vance et al. 2003). However, we found no impairment on the tasks used to assess executive function in the current study. Although the performance accuracy of children with ADHD was lower on the tasks of executive function (working memory and complex matching tasks), these group differences did not reach statistical significance. The magnitude of impairment was, however, moderate ($ds < 0.54$), suggesting this may have been due to insufficient statistical power. The tasks that are typically employed to investigate executive dysfunction in children with ADHD vary greatly, but often include the WCST (Seidman et al. 1997; Houghton et al. 1999; Klorman et al. 1999), TOL (Aman et al. 1998; Nigg et al. 2002; Sonuga-Barke et al. 2002) or the spatial working memory task from the CANTAB battery (SWM; Barnett et al. 2005). We did not use such tests because we considered them inappropriate for the detection of change within a study that repeatedly assessed cognition using brief test-retest intervals. Future studies should examine newly developed measures of executive function for children that are suitable for repeated administration. This is important because executive dysfunction is known to be associated with increased academic and social difficulties (Clark et al. 2002).

One limitation of this study design was that the children, their parents and the assessor were always aware of medication status and the specific dose administered. In order to blind people completely to the medication status, the current design could be modified so that the drug (at different doses) or placebo were not identifiable and then randomised. Such measures were not taken within the current study, as we primarily sought to determine the practicality and statistical power of the design for assessing the effects of medication on symptoms and behaviour. The overall findings of this study demonstrate the design to be a novel, effective method for doing so.

REFERENCES

Achenbach TM. (ed). *Manual for the Child Behaviour Checklist / 4-18 and 1991 Profile.* University of Vermont Department of Psychiatry: Burlington VT, 1991.

Aman MG, Turbott SH. 1991. Prediction of clinical response in children taking methylphenidate. *J. Autism. Dev. Disord.* 21: 211-228.

Aman CJ, Roberts RJ, Pennington BF. 1998. A neuropsychological examination of the underlying deficit in Attention Deficit Hyperactivity Disorder: Frontal lobe versus right parietal lobe theories. *Develop. Psychol.* 34: 956-969.

American Psychiatric Association. (ed). *Diagnostic and Statistical Manual of Mental Disorders, Fourth edition.* Author: Washington DC, 1994.

Barkley RA, DuPaul GJ, McMurray MB. 1991. Attention Deficit Disorder with and without Hyperactivity: Clinical response to three dose levels of methylphenidate. *Pediatrics.* 87: 519-531.

Barkley RA, McMurray MD, Edelbrock CS, Robbins BA. 1989. The response of aggressive and nonaggressive ADHD children to two doses of methylphenidate. *J. Am. Acad. Child Adol. Psychiatry.* 28: 873-888.

Barnett R, Vance A, Maruff P, Luk SL, Costin J, Pantelis C. 2001. Abnormal executive function in attention deficit hyperactivity disorder: The effect of stimulant medication and age on spatial working memory. *Psychol. Med.* 31: 1107-1115.

Barnett R, Maruff P, Vance A, Wood K, Costin J, Luk E. submitted. Executive and cognitive dysfunction in ADHD. *ANZ J. Psychiatry.*

Basso M R, Bornstein R A, Lang J M. 1999. Practice effects of commonly used measures of executive function across twelve months. *Clin. Neuropsychol.* 13: 283-292.

Bedard AC, Ickowicz A, Logan GD, Hogg-Johnson S, Schachar R, Tannock R. 2003. Selective inhibition in children with Attention-Deficit Hyperactivity Disorder off and on stimulant medication. *J. Abnorm. Child Psychol.* 31: 315-327.

Bergman A, Winters L, Cornblatt B. 1991. Methylphenidate: Effects on sustained attention. In *Ritalin: Theory & Patient Management,* Greenhill L, Osman B (eds). Maryann Liebert: New York; 223-231.

Bland JM, Altman DG. 1996. Statistical notes: Measurement error. *Br. Med. J.* 313: 744.

Brodeur DA, Pond M. 2001. The development of selective attention in children with Attention Deficit Hyperactivity Disorder. *J. Abn. Child Psych.* 29: 229-239.

Buitelaar JK, van der Gaag RJ, Swaab-Barneveld H, Kuiper M. 1995. Prediction of clinical response to methylphenidate in children with Attention-Deficit Hyperactivity Disorder. *J. Am. Acad. Child Adolesc. Psychiatry.* 34: 1025-1032.

Cairney S, Maruff P, Vance A, Barnett R, Luk E, Currie J. 2001. Contextual abnormalities of saccadic inhibition in children with attention deficit hyperactivity disorder. *Exp. Brain Res.* 141: 507-518.

Castellanos FX, Tannock R. 2002. Neuroscience of Attention-Deficit/Hyperactivity Disorder: the search for endophenotypes. *Nat. Rev. Neurosci.* 3: 617-628.

Clark C, Prior M, Kinsella G. 2002. The relationship between executive function abilities, adaptive behaviour, and academic achievement in children with externalising behaviour problems. *J. Child Psychol. Psychiatry.* 43: 785-796.

Clarke AR, Barry RJ, Bond D, McCarthy R, Selikowitz M. 2002. Effects of stimulant medications on the EEG of children with Attention-Deficit/Hyperactivity Disorder. *Psychopharm.* 164: 277-284.

Cohen J. 1988. Statistical power for the behavioural sciences 2nd ed., Hilsdale, NJ, Lawrence Erlbaum.

Collie A, Darby DG, Falleti MG, Silbert BS, Maruff P. 2002. Determining the extent of cognitive change after coronary surgery: a review of statistical procedures. *Ann. Thorac. Surg.* 73: 2005-2011.

Collie A, Maruff P, McStephen M, Darby DG. 2003. The effects of practice on the cognitive test performance of neurologically normal individuals assessed at brief test-retest intervals. *J. Int. Neuropsychol. Soc.* 9: 419-428.

Collie A, Maruff P, Makdissi M, McCrory P, McStephen M, Darby D. 2003. CogSport: reliability and correlation with conventional cognitive tests used in post-concussion medical evaluations. *Clin. J. Sport Med.* 13: 28-32.

Conners CK. 1985. Parent Symptom Questionnaire. *Psychopharmacology.* 21: 816-822.

Conners C K. 1997. *Conners' Rating Scales, revised.* New York, Multi-Health Systems.

Conners CK. 2002. Forty years of methylphenidate treatment in Attention-Deficit/Hyperactivity Disorder. *Journal of Attention Disorders.* 5: S17-S30.

Conners CK, Epstein JN, March JS, Angold A, Wells K, Klaric J, Swanson JM, Arnold LE, Abikoff HB, Elliot GR, Greenhill LL, Hechtman L, Hinshaw SP, Hoza B, Jensen PS, Kraemer HC, Newcorn JH, Pelham WE, Severe JB, Vitiello B, & Wigal T. 2001. Multimodal treatment of ADHD in the MAT: an alternative outcome analysis. *J. Am. Acad. Child Adolesc. Psychiatry.* 40: 159-167.

Denney CB, Rapport MD. 1999. Predicting methylphenidate response in children with ADHD: Theoretical empirical and conceptual models. *J Am Acad. Child Adolesc. Psychiatry.* 38: 393-401.

Denney C B, Rapport M D. 2001. Cognitive Pharmacology of Stimulants in children with ADHD. In: *Stimulant Drugs and ADHD.* Edited by Solanto MV, Arnsten AFT, Castellanos FX. Oxford, Oxford University Press, pp 283-302.

de Sonneville LMJ, Njiokiktjien C, Bos H. 1994. Methylphenidate and information processing. Part 1: differentiation between responders and nonresponders; Part 2: efficacy in responders. *J. Clin. Exp. Neuropsychol.* 16: 877-897.

Douglas VI. 1999. Cognitive control processes in Attention-Deficit Hyperactivity Disorder. In *Handbook of Disruptive Behaviour Disorders,* Quay HC, Hogan AE. (eds). Plenum Press: New York; 105-138.

Douglas VI, Barr RG, Desilets J, Sherman E. 1995. Do high doses of stimulants impair flexible thinking in Attention-Deficit Hyperactivity Disorder? *J. Am. Acad. Child Adolesc. Psychiatry.* 34: 877-885.

Douglas VI, Barr RG, O'Neill ME, Britton BG. 1986. Short term effects of methylphenidate on the cognitive learning and academic performance of children with Attention Deficit Disorder in the laboratory and the classroom. *J. Child Psychol. Psychiatry.* 27: 191-211.

Dunlap WP, Cortina JM, Vaslow JB, Burke MJ. 1996. Meta-Analysis of experiments with matched groups or repeated measures designs. *Psychol. Methods.* 1: 170-177.

DuPaul G, Barkley RA, McMurray MB. 1994. Response of children with ADHD to methylphenidate: Interaction with internalizing symptoms. *J. Am. Acad. Child Adolesc. Psychiatry.* 33: 894-903.

Efron D, Jarman F, Barker M. 1997. Methylphenidate versus dexamphetamine in children with Attention Deficit Hyperactivity Disorder: A double-blind crossover trial. *Pediatrics.* 100: E6.

Elia J, Borcherding BG, Rapoport JL, Keysor CS. 1991. Methylphenidate and dextroamphetamine treatments of hyperactivity: Are there true nonresponders? *Psychiatry Res.* 36: 141-155.

Elliott R, Sahakian BJ, Matthews K, Bannerjea A, Rimmer J, Robbins TW. 1997. Effects of methylphenidate on spatial working memory and planning in healthy young adults. *Psychopharm.* 131: 196-206.

Evans RW, Gualtieri CT, Amara I. 1986. Methylphenidate and memory: dissociated effects in hyperactive children. *Psychopharm.* 90: 211-216.

Falleti MG, Maruff P, Collie A, Darby DG, McStephen, M. 2003. Qualitative similarities in cognitive impairment associated with 24 hours of sustained wakefulness and a blood alcohol concentration of 0.05%. *J. Sleep Res.* 12: 265-274.

Gittelman-Klein R, Klein DF. 1975. Are behavioural and psychometric changes related in methylphenidate-treated, hyperactive children? *Int. J. Men Health.* 4: 182-198.

Gittelman-Klein R, Klein DF. 1976. Methylphenidate effects in learning disabilities. *Arch. Gen. Psychiatry.* 33: 655-664.

Gray JR, Kagan J. 2000. The challenge of predicting which children with Attention Deficit-Hyperactivity Disorder will respond positively to methylphenidate. *J. Appl. Dev. Psychol.* 21: 471-489.

Greenberg LM, Waldman ID. 1993. Developmental normative data on the test of variables of attention (T.O.V.A.). *J. Child Psychol. Psychiatry.* 34: 1019-1030.

Greenhill LL. 2001. Clinical effects of stimulant medication in ADHD. In *Stimulant drugs and ADHD*, Solanto MN, Arnsten AFT, Castellanos FX (eds). Oxford University Press: New York; 31-71.

Hoagwood K, Kelleher KJ, Feil MMS, Comer DM. 2000. Treatment services for children with ADHD: A national perspective. *J. Am. Acad. Child Adolesc. Psychiatry.* 39: 198-206.

Hopkins WG. 2003. A new view of statistics (On-line). Available: www.sportsci.org/resource/stats/index.html. Accessed December 2003.

Houghton S, Douglas G, West J, Whiting K, Wall M, Langsford S, Powell L, Caroll A. 1999. Differential patterns of executive function in children with attention-deficit hyperactivity disorder according to gender and subtype. *J. Child Neurol.* 14: 801-805.

Ingraham LJ, Aitken CB. 1996. An empirical approach to determining criteria for abnormality in test batteries with multiple measures. *Neuropsychology.* 10: 120-124.

Jacobson NS, Traux P. 1991. Clinical significance: a statistical approach to defining meaningful change in psychotherapy research. *J. Consult. Clin. Psychol.* 59: 12-19.

Kempton S, Vance A, Maruff P, Luk E, Costin E, Pantelis C. 1999. Executive function and attention deficit hyperactivity disorder: stimulant medication and better executive function performance in children. *Psychol. Med.* 29: 527-538.

Kent MA, Camfield CS, Camfield PR. 1999. Double-blind methylphenidate trials: practical useful and highly endorsed by families. *Arch. Pediatr. Adolesc. Med.* 153: 1292-1296.

Klein DF. 2008. The loss of serendipity in psychopharmacology. *JAMA.* 299: 1063-1065.

Klorman R, Hazel-Fernandez LA, Shaywitz SE, Fletcher JM, Marchione KE, Holahan JM, Stuebing KK, Shaywitz BA. 1999. Executive functioning deficits in attention-deficit/hyperactivity disorder are independent of oppositional defiant or reading disorder. *J. Am. Acad. Child Adol. Psychiatry.* 38: 1148-1155.

Maruff P, Currie J, Pantelis C, Smith D. 1996. Deficits in the endogenous control of covert attention in chronic schizophrenia. *Neuropsychologia.* 34: 1079-1084.

McCaffrey R J, Westervelt H J. 1995. Issues associated with repeated neuropsychological assessments. *Neuropsych. Rev.* 5: 203-221.

Mehta M, Goodyear IM, Sahakian BJ. 2004. Methylphenidate improves working memory and set shifting in ADHD: relationships to baseline memory capacity. *J. Child Psychol. Psychiatry.* 45: 293-305.

Mollica CM, Maruff P, Collie A, Vance A. 2005. The effects of age and practice on the consistency of performance on a computerized assessment of cognitive change in children. *J. Child Neuropsychol.* 11: 303-310.

Mollica CM, Maruff P, Vance A, Collie A, submitted. The effects of stimulant medication on the cognitive and behavioural function of children with attention-deficit/hyperactivity disorder- combined type (ADHD-CT). *ANZ J. Psychiatry.*

Nigg JT, Blaskey LG, Huang-Pollock CL, Rappley MD. 2002. Neuropsychological executive functions and DSM-IV ADHD subtypes. *J. Am. Acad. Child Adolesc. Psychiatry.* 41: 59-66.

O'Toole K, Abramowitz A, Morris R, Duclan M. 1997. Effects of methylphenidate on attention and nonverbal learning in children with Attention-Deficit Hyperactivity Disorder. *J. Am. Acad. Child Adol. Psychiatry.* 36: 531-538.

Paule MG, Rowland AS, Ferguson SA, Chelonis JJ, Tannock R, Swanson JM, Castellanos FX. 2000. Attention Deficit/Hyperactivity Disorder: Characteristics interventions and models. *Neurotoxicol. Teratol.* 22: 631-351.

Pennington BF, Ozonoff S. 1996. Executive functions and developmental psychopathology. *J. Child Psychol. Psychiatry.* 37: 51-87.

Pietrzak RH, Mollica CM, Maruff P, Snyder PJ. 2006. Cognitive effects of immediate release methylphenidate in children with ADHD. *Neurosci. Biobehav. Rev.* 30: 1225-1245.

Rapport MD, Denney CB. 2000. Attention Deficit Hyperactivity Disorder and methylphenidate: assessment and prediction of clinical response. In *Ritalin: Theory and Practice*, Greenhill LL, Osman BB (eds). Mary Ann Liebert: Larchmont NY; 45-70.

Rapport MD, Kelly KL. 1993. Psychostimulant effects on learning and cognitive function. In *Handbook of Hyperactivity in Children*, Matson JL (ed). Allyn & Bacon: Boston; 97-136.

Rasmussen LS, Larsen K, Houx P, Skovgaard LT, Hanning CD, Moller JT. 2001. The assessment of postoperative cognitive function. *Acta Anaesthesiol. Scand.* 45: 275-289.

Reynolds CR, Richmond BO. 1978. What I Think and Feel: a revised measure of the children's manifest anxiety. *J. Abn. Child Psychol.* 6: 271-280.

Rodgers J, Marckus R, Kearns P, Windebank K. 2003. Attentional ability among survivors of leukaemia treated without cranial irradiation. *Arch. Dis. Child.* 88: 147-150.

Rutter M, Graham P. 1968. The reliability and validity of the psychiatric assessment of the child: I. Interview with the child. *Br. J. Psychiatry.* 114: 563-579.

Santosh PJ, Taylor E. 2000. Stimulant Drugs. *Eur. Child Adol. Psychiatry.* 9: I/27 - I/43.

Scheres A, Oosterlaan J, Swanson J, Morein-Zamir S, Meiran N, Schut H, Vlasveld L,
Sergeant JA. 2003. The effect of methylphenidate on three forms of response inhibition in boys with AD/HD. *J. Abn. Child Psychol.* 31: 105-120.

Seidman LJ, Biederman J, Faraone SV, Weber W, Oullette C. 1997. Toward defining a neuropsychology of attention deficit-hyperactivity disorder: performance of children and adolescents from a large clinically referred sample. *J. Consul. Clin. Psychol.* 65: 150-160.

Shallice T, Marzocchi GM, Coser S, Del Savio M, Meuter RF, Rumiatia RI. 2002. Executive function profile of children with Attention Deficit Hyperactivity Disorder. *Dev. Neuropsych.* 21: 43-71.

Silbert BS, Maruff P, Evered LA, Scott DA, Kalpokas M, Martin KJ, Lewis MS, Myles PS. 2004. Detection of cognitive decline after coronary surgery: A comparison of computerised and conventional tests. *Br. J. Anaesth.* 92: 814-820.

Silverman WK, Albano AM. 1996. *Anxiety Disorders Interview Schedule for Children (DSM-IV)*. Texas, Graywind.

Sonuga-Barke EJ, Dalen L, Daley D, Remington B. 2002. Are planning, working memory, and inhibition associated with individual differences in preschool ADHD symptoms? *Dev. Neuropsychol.* 21: 255-272.

Sprague RL, Sleator EK. 1977. Methylphenidate in hyperkinetic children: Differences in dose effects on learning and social behaviour. *Science.* 198: 1274-1276.

Swanson JM, Kinsbourne M, Roberts W, Zucker K. 1978. Time-response analysis of stimulant medication on the learning ability of children referred for hyperactivity. *Pediatrics.* 61: 21-29.

Swanson JM, Cantwell D, Lerner M, McBurnett K, Hanna G. 1991. Effects of stimulant medication on learning in children with ADHD. *J. Learning Disab.* 24: 219-230.

Swanson JM, McBurnett K, Wigal T, Pfiffner LJ, Williams L, Christian DL. 1993. Effects of stimulant medication on children with attention deficit disorder: A 'review of reviews'. *Exceptional Children.* 60: 154-162.

Tannock R, Schachar R. 1992. Methylphenidate and cognitive perseveration in hyperactive children. *J. Child Psychol. Psychiatry.* 33: 1217-1228.

Tannock R, Ickowicz A, Schachar R. 1995. Differential effects of methylphenidate on working memory in ADHD children with and without comorbid anxiety. *J. Am. Acad. Child Adolesc. Psychiatry.* 34: 886-896.

Taylor E, Schachar R, Thorley G, Wieselberg HM, Everitt B, Rutter M. 1987. Which boys respond to stimulant medication? A controlled trial of methylphenidate in boys with disruptive behaviour. *Psychol. Med.* 17: 121-143.

Uhlenhuth EH, Turner DA, Purchatzke G, Gift T, Chassan J. 1977. Intensive design in evaluating anxiolytic agents. *Psychopharm. (Berl)* 52: 79-85.

Vance A, Barnett R. 2002. *Children's Impulsiveness Scale.* Melbourne, Australia, Alfred Hospital.

Vance A, Maruff P, Barnett R. 2003. Attention Deficit Hyperactivity Disorder, combined type (ADHD-CT): better executive function performance with longer-term psychostimulant medication. *A. N. Z. J. Psychiatry.* 37: 570-576.

Wechsler D. 2004. *Wechsler Intelligence Scale for Children, 4th ed.* San Antonio TX, Psychological Corporation.

Winer BJ (ed). *Statistical Principles in Experimental Design.* McGraw-Hill: London, 1971.

Wood K, Maruff P, Farrow M, Levy F, Hay D. 1999. Covert orienting of visual attention in children with attention deficit disorder: Does comorbidity make a difference? *Arch. Neuropsychol.* 14: 179-189.

INDEX